To Murray & Alan

Happy New Year

Much love

Mindie

Years ago, I went to Chicago and had the opportunity to meet Victor Skrebneski.
Immediately I felt a strong sympathy with him and discovered his great talent.
Victor Skrebneski has the genius of photography.
The human being which Victor Skrebneski is, is as important to me as his talent and
shines with strength and beauty.
Victor, thank you for all this beauty you have given us. Thank you for being my
friend. I will be always grateful for this . . .

HUBERT DE GIVENCHY
1 March 1995

Fashion is, by its nature, a perilous way of life.

EMANUEL UNGARO
22 September 1994

The Art of HAUTE COUTURE

PHOTOGRAPHS BY
VICTOR SKREBNESKI

TEXT BY
LAURA JACOBS

ABBEVILLE PRESS · PUBLISHERS · NEW YORK · LONDON · PARIS

JACKET FRONT: Karl Lagerfeld for Chanel, 1989: Detail of fitted, slipper-satin dinner suit, deeply beaded and embroidered (see also pages 116 and 117). JACKET BACK: Galanos, 1994: Double-layered bias-cut pale pink silk satin gown with bra top made with crystals and pale pink caviar beads (see also pages 107 and 108). FRONTIS-PIECE: Givenchy, 1991: Black tulle gown strapped and bowed in black velvet, and sprinkled with black paillettes (see also pages 120 and 121). PAGE 6: Geoffrey Beene, 1995: Silver panne velvet "Mercury" dress. Dresses on pages 10, 11, 12, 15, 16, 18, and 19 courtesy of the Hope B. McCormick Costume Center at the Chicago Historical Society.

Editor: JACQUELINE DECTER
Designer: MOLLY SHIELDS
Typesetter: BARBARA STURMAN

Production Editor: OWEN DUGAN
Production Manager: LOUIS BILKA

Photographs copyright © 1995 Victor Skrebneski. Text and compilation, including selection of text and images, copyright © 1995 Abbeville Press, Inc. All rights reserved under international copyright conventions. No part of this book may be reproduced or utilized in any form or by any means, electronic or mechanical, including photocopying, recording, or by any information storage and retrieval system, without permission in writing from the publisher. Inquiries should be addressed to Abbeville Publishing Group, 488 Madison Avenue, New York, NY 10022. The text of this book was set in Slanted Antique Roman. Printed and bound in Italy. First edition

2   4   6   8   10   9   7   5   3   1

Library of Congress Cataloging-in-Publication Data
Skrebneski, Victor.
The art of haute couture / photographs by Victor Skrebneski ; text by Laura Jacobs.
p.   cm.
Includes bibliographical references and index.
ISBN 0-7892-0022-8
1. Fashion photography. 2. Fashion—Pictorial works.
3. Skrebneski, Victor. I. Jacobs, Laura. II. Title.
TR679.S569   1995
779'.974692—dc20   95-21225

This book is dedicated to my dear friend Hubert de Givenchy, who was my inspiration
long before we met and continues to be that inspiration in every aspect of my life.
I also dedicate this book to cherished friends Mary Louise Norton,
Frank Zachary, and Nancy Tuck Gardiner.

SKREBNESKI
1 May 1995

CONTENTS

It all began with a Rose. Her name was Rose Bertin, and in the middle of the eighteenth century she arrived in Paris, apprentice to the milliner Pagalle. In 1771, when she was twenty-seven and already a darling of the court, she was introduced to a new, shy arrival, the Dauphine Marie-Antoinette, a sixteen-year-old from Austria who had yet to define herself or her style, but had been advised by her mother to set the fashion, never to follow it. With Rose's counsel in hats, hair, and court attire, Marie-Antoinette blossomed into a sophisticate, becoming the world's most emulated woman (Let them wear ribbons!). Bertin herself was soon known as Minister of Fashion, a fitting title for the only person, man or woman, allowed entry into Versailles without a pass.

Technically speaking, Bertin was more a consultant than a couturier: instead of imposing a diva vision on clothes of her own design, she worked with her clients in a spirit of collaboration. And yet Rose Bertin qualifies as the first name in fashion history, for her story possesses all the key elements of that much larger, longer story. There is the muse of flesh and blood, and the embodiment of an era and its ideals through cloth and cut. There is also the easy association with royalty and wealth; the creation of a high style that enchants the masses; and the cultivation of beauty in a Paris locale. These are the leitmotifs of haute couture, a business known by those who practice it as "the art of perfection," and more simply understood as the world of the Paris original.

The official beginnings of haute couture are found in the next century, bound up in the destiny of an Englishman. Charles Frederick Worth began his career in the draper's trade in London, but left for Paris in 1845, drawn there by the city's fabled mystique. Employed at the Parisian company of Gagelin and Opigez, he began making dresses for his wife, Marie, a fellow worker, and the admiring attention these

SUITABLY STATUESQUE,
JACQUELINE DE RIBES MODELS
A GOWN OF HER OWN DESIGN
AMID CONSTRUCTION AT
THE MUSÉE DES ARTS
DÉCORATIFS, PARIS, 1983.

received posed a question. Why not expand into dressmaking? Worth convinced his employers that this could be a natural and lucrative extension of the fine-stuffs business. His success was immediate, and after ten years of behind-the-scenes designing, he left in 1858 to open his own company: the house of Worth. As Bertin had her queen, so Worth had his empress. She came to him through Princess Pauline de Metternich, wife of an Austrian ambassador, who wore a Worth to court and caught the most important eye in the room—that of Empress Eugénie, wife of Napoleon III. When Eugénie requested a meeting with the couturier, his name was made. Any woman who would be chic took herself to 7, rue de la Paix, where feted and fitted she became worth her weight in Worth.

Worth's approach to fashion is a fascinating essay in sumptuous display and somewhat expedient design. Silhouette changed slowly, and his was an art of ornamentation, infinite variations on a crinolined, then corseted theme. But Worth was in control. It was he who dictated the changes, his vision taking precedence over a client's wrongheaded whim. And it was he who lasted. The house of Worth retained its luster even as the aristocrats it dressed were drummed out of power. This autonomy and leadership set a new standard for dressmakers. After Worth, couture was no longer an echelon of anonymous tradespeople, but a galaxy of stars.

Worth's stress on aesthetic control was not the only standard he set. It was at Worth that the couture house hierarchy was established, and it was very much like the structure at the great opera and ballet companies. If classical dance had its apprentice corps girls, nicknamed

THE BUSTLED SILHOUETTE OF
WORTH IS REFLECTED IN THIS
NINETEENTH-CENTURY TRIO OF
TROUSSEAU DRESSES FASHIONED
(LEFT TO RIGHT) IN GRAY SILK
TAFFETA, IRIDESCENT PINK TAFFETA,
AND GRAY SILK FAILLE (ABOVE).
CHICAGO DRESSMAKER ADA F.
MOORE IS BELIEVED TO HAVE
MADE THIS PINK PLEATED GOWN
IN 1898 (FACING PAGE).

"rats," couture had its arpettes, nicknamed "rabbits," apprentices
who originally picked up the pins but today act as runners between the
house's various floors. The ballet had, in ascending order, coryphées,
soloists, and ballerinas; the couture house, its premières mains
qualifiées and deuxièmes mains qualifiées (first- and second-level
seamstresses, teamed as pairs in the workrooms), its fitters (the head
of each workroom), its vendeuses and secondes vendeuses (ambas-
sadors of the salon, each with her own jealously guarded clientele and
equally guarded relationships with the fitters). Like a little principality,
the structure was a pyramid shape with the designer at the top, balanc-
ing on a pinpoint or, rather, on the directrice, the designer's right hand,
the woman in charge of pricing dresses, handling accounts with manufacturers, and the all around running of the house.

   During the Age of Worth, another lasting structure was put
into place: the Chambre Syndicale de la Couture Parisienne. Though

The Art of Haute Couture ⌐ 11

the organization dates back to 1868, when it was a union that presided over France's various needle trades, it acquired its title in 1885, when Gaston Worth (son of Charles Frederick) realized that the growing competition among couturiers required a more specific and coherent management. Part guild, part union, the Chambre set forth the criteria that won a designer haute couture status. It also took over such sticky, even volatile, concerns as labor relations, the coordination of collections (who shows when within what time period), the registration and monitoring of international store buyers and foreign press, the direction of the Chambre Syndicale schools, and the passing of financial regulations (in 1914, for instance, an effort to ensure cash flow decreed that gowns be paid for not at delivery, but upon order).

Perhaps the most frustrating and intriguing of the Chambre's many challenges has been the looming problem of piracy—an issue that goes to the heart of haute couture. For not only is Paris fashion a

EMMA AND HELENE PIEDERIT OF CHICAGO CREATED THIS BLACK TULLE AND GOLD PAILLETTE EVENING GOWN IN 1916, A TIME WHEN THE WAR KEPT AMERICANS FROM BUYING IN PARIS.

business of constant evolution and imaginative flight, it has been for much of its history the most authoritative of art forms, the last and only word. Inspiration might come from the stage, or from other cultures, or from a stylish wife, model, or muse, or from a bolt of amazing material, but the look was designed in, stitched together in, and presented in Paris. Every dress was a first, a secret formula that the fashionable—rich and less rich alike—were going to want as soon as possible. Theft, obviously, was faster and cheaper than the elaborate process of after-show, in-house appointments and paid-for patterns and dresses. Hence the hidden cameras, the spylike sketching, the photographic memories.

Most couturiers understand that with time dressmakers in many countries will be copying their work. Such is the logical outcome of any innovation or new trend. Some designers even embraced the copyists. One of the reasons Coco Chanel never joined the Chambre was because she felt it was hypocritical to set a style and then treat it as a state secret. Still, express distinctions were made between innocent "trickle down" and big-business plagiarism. Eventually, every dress designed by one of the Chambre's members was registered before the showing in a file that included a sketch, photograph, and fabric swatch.

Indeed, Paris couture was so high and mighty and, it might be said, dictatorial, that Hitler himself wanted it. During the first years of the Occupation of France, the Germans decided that the couture capital should move to Vienna or Berlin, and only the unflagging resistance of Madame Grès and the perfect reasoning of Chambre president Lucien LeLong—his tautology being that Paris couture could not exist outside Paris—convinced Goebbels to leave it be. In fact, haute couture has an enviable record in the never-say-die department. Not only has it not closed down during any war—an admission of defeated morale that might have more impact on the world than you think—it was actually defiant during the Occupation. Creating clothes that were increasingly frivolous and absurd, designers decreed purposeful waste and whimsy the uniform of patriotic Frenchwomen, an unmistakable nose-thumbing at the invaders who might steal resources but could not steal souls. The minute the war was over, the Chambre instituted strict, temporary rationing of these same materials; they were French again, and needed elsewhere.

Today, the terms for membership in the Chambre fit on one page of paper. There are ten short sections, and key among them are the following stipulations. Patterns must be exclusively created by the fashion designer or the designer's team of permanent modelists (no free-lance help), and must be made in the firm's own workshops. These workshops must employ a minimum of twenty people, with a production staff that includes premières and secondes d'atelier (vendeuses), premières and secondes mains. The collections are to be presented twice a year in Paris on dates set by the Chambre, each collection composed of not less than seventy-five patterns and presented on at least three living models. In addition to the showing with the Chambre, the fashion house must also present the collection forty-five times on its own premises. Finally, the patterns duplicated by the firm can only be made to the measurements of the clients: "No mass production."

These rules may sound purely technical—a list of numerical cut-offs and schedule requirements—but they are founded on convictions that go much deeper. Built into the Chambre's specifications is a structure of permanent relationships that form the philosophical heart of the house: each link is equally essential, and each person, from seamstress to vendeuse to model to delivery boy, plays a part in the dress's final flawlessness. The seasonal polarity of fall/winter and spring/summer suggests couture's eternal round, the way it is forever

THREE GOWNS FROM THE 1930S FORM A PAS DE TROIS THAT INCLUDES (LEFT TO RIGHT) A BLACK SILK CREPE FROM FRANCE, A RUFFLED ORGANDY MADE IN AMERICA, AND A HARLEQUINED ORGANZA BY THE FLAMBOYANT NEW YORK DESIGNER VALENTINA, A RUSSIAN ÉMIGRÉ.

six months ahead of the rest of the world, leading into the future. Encoded as well is an ethic: the extra-human effort demanded by the "handmade," the implicit time requirement of the three to five personal fittings that fulfill the commandment of "no mass production." In what other discipline is a work of art taken apart and put back together again at least three times as a matter of course? It is said that Cristóbal Balenciaga could dismantle a jacket with his thumbs.

"Am I a fool when I dream of putting art in my dresses, a fool when I say dressmaking is an art?" asked Paul Poiret in his autobiography King of Fashion, a rhetorical question to which the obvious answer is "No!" Couturiers themselves have rarely doubted their position as artists. While a designer can come to fashion straight from home— Balenciaga began his phenomenal career as a boy with no special training, and Emanuel Ungaro worked in his father's tailoring business until he was twenty-two, then apprenticed with Balenciaga—many a designer begins his or her career in one of the other arts: Madame Grès trained as a musician and sculptor, Mainbocher was an opera singer, Valentino studied architecture. An eye for line, a love of the stuff of fashion (fabric, laces, buttons, trim), and plain old fate lead them to couture. Not surprisingly, architecture was the first choice for quite a few men who went on to the fashion world. Perhaps Christian Dior, whose parents prevented him from its study, and who liked to ally himself with modernists and cubists rather than with the more unconstructed late-Romantics, made the connection best when he said, "I think of my work as ephemeral architecture, glorifying the proportions of the female body."

Meanwhile, Coco Chanel used to snipe at the well-educated Elsa Schiaparelli by calling her "that Italian artist who makes dresses," a slap against Schiap's couture status that simultaneously acknowledges

THIS SHEATH-AND-BELL-SHAPED DRESS, DESIGNED IN 1913 BY A YOUNG ERTÉ FOR THE HOUSE OF PAUL POIRET, RINGS IN THE TWENTIETH CENTURY.

her undeniable imagination, her collaborations with Christian Bérard

and Salvador Dali. Chanel herself had rubbed shoulders with some of

the greatest artists of the twentieth century—Stravinsky, Balanchine,

Colette—and their aesthetic rubbed off. Rather than tempt the muse with

grandiose statements, these artists paid homage to humility, concentrat-

ing on craft and technique and the measurements of the job at hand. The

humility could get a bit thick, however, for though Chanel might demur

at the term "artist," she held forth on fashion and life like la divina.

Those who took their role as artist too seriously could run into trouble. The brilliant American Charles James, remembered best for his satin gowns, stiff as baked meringue, really did treat each piece as art. Like a sculptor who keeps chipping away, or a painter forever daubing, he would take a dress apart over and over again, often missing the delivery date. Caught up in his genius as if in a cult, his clients, the most stylish women in the world, endured this caprice and ended up borrowing James dresses from each other. At the time of his death, he was obsessively documenting his limited life's work. James's opposite might be a designer like Madeleine Vionnet, who had less art in her difficult background than any other designer at the turn of the century. Many of her peers felt, and designers today still feel, that she was the greatest couturier of all (those who disagree put Balenciaga on top). Her work—instinctual, utterly fluid—was uncopiable, and it is one of history's unique losses that not one of her incomparable drape dresses is known to survive today. Her view of herself was no-nonsense: first, she was an artist; second, a businesswoman.

THE BROWN LINEN DRESS

Several months before, Cristóbal Balenciaga had announced that he would close his Maison de Couture in Paris and retire to his native Spain.

For ten years he had made almost everything I wore . . . from elegant déshabilles to nightgowns and fine batiste petticoats. I was brought to his house on Avenue George V by my close friend, Jean Schlumberger. They were friends, and at times Cristóbal handed his pencil over to Johnny.

Many dresses and suits were the work of both men . . . not because I was a fashion plate, but they understood my need was often a simple working fashion with interest in all aspects of gardens and life in the country as well as ballgowns, evening coats and extraordinary hats. So, it was a sad but compelling thing for me to stop late one summer afternoon, before leaving for Virginia the next day, to embrace this dear man.

Arriving in his tiny elevator with Mademoiselle Renée, I found him wandering about his studio floor. All the pancartes covered with extraordinary samples of fabrics, colors, buttons, ribbons, feathers, etc., were gone. An almost empty rack was left that held the uniforms he had designed for the personnel and stewardesses of Air France.

"Your dress is too large on the shoulders, Bunny," were his words of greeting. "Call Felicia." Felicia was his premier fitter.

By the time she arrived my dress was off and I was sitting in a model's white smock. He had sent for scissors, needle and thread.

"What are your plans?" I asked. "First, I am going to remake these shoulders," was his reply. Much of his charm lay in his eyes, a combination of gentleness and humor. His hands were small and moved quickly. Over his glasses he would look at me as we talked. Then his eyes went back to the brown sleeveless linen dress. "You are pulling it apart, Monsieur," Felicia said to him. They both spoke a broken French with a Spanish accent on my behalf that did not always help my understanding of the language.

The light was fading as I watched my dress come apart. Finally, at nearly dark he said, "Felicia, have you one of Madame Mellon's blue jean skirts that she brought for me to copy?" "Oui, Monsieur." "Bring it down. She can wear it with one of the Air France blouses to go home." Taking a blouse from the rack, the thimble still on his finger, he said, "Try this."

My old skirt arrived . . . It had been in the atelier for ten or more years. I put it on. He stood back and looked at me. Then taking me by both shoulders he said,

BALENCIAGA'S BROWN LINEN DRESS FOR
BUNNY MELLON, 1968.

"Now you leave exactly as you arrived . . . nothing here has changed your character." There were tears in both our eyes. "Come see me in Spain." He kissed me three times. "We will send your dress tomorrow."

I was alone in the little elevator. A watchman opened the door on the ground floor and let me out into the street. The street lamps were lit. As I got into the car I looked back. The heavy iron shutters clattered down. The shop of the man I admired was closed shut. I would never see it with him in it again. The choked feeling stayed a long time. He understood that beautiful dresses never changed the inner human truth. This is what he believed in and loved.

The brown dress arrived before ten o'clock the next morning. Cristóbal had remade it himself.

Bunny Mellon
September 1994

BALENCIAGA WAS AN INSPIRATION NOT ONLY TO DESIGNERS BUT TO THE WOMEN HE DESIGNED FOR. WHEN THE MASTER CLOSED HIS HOUSE IN 1968, HE SENT LONGTIME CLIENT BUNNY MELLON TO A YOUNG TALENT HE HAD NURTURED, GIVENCHY. PICTURED HERE IS A PURPLE SUEDE EVENING COAT WITH APPLIQUÉD MIRÓ ABSTRACTIONS—BY GIVENCHY FOR BUNNY (BELOW). ONE OF THE MOST FAMOUS DRESSES IN HOLLYWOOD HISTORY IS A GIVENCHY GOWN WORN BY AUDREY HEPBURN IN THE 1954 FILM *SABRINA* (FACING PAGE).

"The life which supported couture is finished. Real couture is a luxury which is just impossible to do anymore." So said Balenciaga after he closed his house in 1968, sounding the end of a sublime three-decade reign. He often remarked that he longed to be like a painter—just him and the canvas. It is a comparison that reflects the myriad and wearying contingencies of haute couture: how the designer depends on the fabric and accessories manufacturers, on the staff and the models, on the clientele and the press, and in many cases on the financial backers. The couturier is at the center of it all, a situation that would drive any artist, those souls in solitary pursuit, to distraction. No wonder Christian Dior was always in a panic, and Karl Lagerfeld resides behind fan and shades, and Yves Saint Laurent does a disappearing act. Perhaps the couturier's contentment is found alone with the toile, *that master pattern made up in the colorless muslin that holds shape so well (often better than the final fabric) and is the first "canvas" on which the dress is conceived.*

In every era, the costliest Paris couture item can equal the price of a vacation or a middle-class car (American auto companies used to telephone French textile firms hoping to learn which colors would dominate the season). An original is a luxury that more women have dreamed of than enjoyed firsthand, and those who do own these miracles of construction own them forever. (Pieces of social history, the creations sometimes come out of storage for museum exhibitions; after all, a Jackie Kennedy Givenchy is as telling of White House tones and tensions as an Audrey Hepburn Givenchy is of Hollywood dreaming.) At the same time, haute couture is an ideal that, if not older

than Paris, is ultimately larger, an art that can appear mysteriously and unmistakably anywhere, with or without the Chambre's certification. In Italy, the stark yet soft silhouette of Armani is pure couture, and Versace inches closer with every uninhibited collection. In America, Geoffrey Beene has long been peerless in terms of the exploratory sensation of his seaming, held spellbound by an enigmatic hand finish. He upholds haute couture's standard of impeccable execution, its stress on one-of-a-kind design, as do fellow Americans James Galanos and Arnold Scaasi.

Still, the French have been jealously possessive of their couture and have protected the title as best they can—with good reason. From the start, fashion was fabulous for France. One explanation for why Worth was so slow to alter that bloated, bell-shaped silhouette was because of the dire effect it would have on French textile manufacturers, whose yards and yards of silk were covering not only Worth's big crinolines but big crinolines around the world. Haute couture has never been just dresses; it is fabric, fur, purses, shoes, jewelry, the whole exportable interdependency of fancy and fantasy. By the 1950s, Paris fashion was the second largest export industry in France (steel was first, which says something about the cutting edge of couture).

There was, however, something from which France could not protect haute couture, and that was prêt-à-porter. As ready-to-wear churned out cheaper models, spurring on the democratization of

EACH COUTURIER HAS A PAMPERED AND PEDIGREED CLIENT LIST. THESE GIVENCHYS WERE CREATED FOR CAROLL PETRIE IN 1987 (THE SEQUINED EVENING DRESS LEFT), THE DUCHESS OF WINDSOR IN 1966 (THE SILK ORGANZA DINNER DRESS BELOW), AND FIRST LADY JACQUELINE KENNEDY IN 1961 (THE IVORY ENSEMBLE OPPOSITE).

Each woman is unique, and these three Givenchys consider time, place, and character. The worldly peach crepe gown with fox-trimmed poncho (facing page) was designed for Countess Anita Von Galen in 1973; the dalmation-dotted silk (right) was made up for Anne Bass in 1987; and the sophisticated yellow georgette (below) captures Sao Schlumberger in 1980.

fashion (a designer label on every pocket!), and "up from the streets" became the zeitgeist sneer at trickle-down-from-the-top, couture began to look too slow, too authoritarian, too time-consuming, too expensive, too elitist. These are the classic complaints of the late twentieth century, leveled at everything from the museum to the novel, the ballet company to the King's English, and yes, at the couturier too. By the early 1980s haute couture had dropped to eighth on the list of exports. The houses made most of their money on licenses—perfume, scarves, handbags— and their couture work was often looked upon as a laboratory of ideas that would then be simplified and sold in their less expensive boutiques.

Balenciaga was wrong about little when it came to his calling, but he was wrong about the end of Paris couture. It is true that every few years a spate of articles tolls the bell for old ways, mourning the loss of the couture clientele. Then comes an economic boom, or the emergence of an exciting new designer, and women again set out in search of the perfect fit, ready for the garment of definitive cut and quality, a design that tells them a little bit about themselves and about the world—what the human hand is capable of making. As we approach the end of this century, couture is blossoming once more, and women have come full circle. The idea of time spent working toward transcendence,

rather than just working, is newly attractive. If mediocrity is the end result of speed and convenience, what's the point?

And while prêt-à-porter may have proved itself a billion-dollar business, and its designers are household names in the way couturiers used to be, it is still, quite simply, not couture. Today's young talents have their heads turned toward Paris, their eyes on the houses of aging masters, their breath held. As Dior première Mme. Marguerite once explained, the difference between haute couture and ready-to-wear resides, symbolically, in the hot iron that sculpts materials into human form: "Shaping materials is something ready-to-wear could not do; they put darts instead." These days, ready-to-wear hardly uses darts, and hot young designers are itching for the iron, intrigued by the old techniques.

Silk and satin do not last like oil on canvas, and besides, how many Picassos have been stained by champagne or a dropped canapé? Trends in fashion cycle swiftly compared to those in symphonic music or opera, where a craze, say verismo, can be in vogue for decades. And yet, a great dress on the right woman can be as important and unforgettable as a great aria on the right soprano. A puritan apology is at work when the love of couture is deemed frivolous, for it is these silhouettes that net the momentary hopes of a generation, catch the atmospheric pressures of sex, class, calm, and chaos, and wrap them in an intimate and knowing bow. Haute couture can claim poetry and dance as sister arts, the first for its accent on hidden interiors and its suit of structure, the second for its stress on a body's shape and will to move, its brightening glance. Haute couture holds perfection and metamorphosis in stunning balance. In that, it stands alone among the arts.

_T_he human eye responds to edges—the boundaries between light and dark that create lines that suggest shapes that become images. Neckline, bustline, waistline, hemline. The terms of tailoring are clear and territorial—scissors have flashed and culture wars been waged over where the lines are drawn, and why the boundaries are crossed. Line is definitive. In the late nineteenth century, the S-bend was the prevailing silhouette, a corsetted shape that could cripple; it was abandoned with a millennial sigh of relief. When Christian Dior began his reign in 1947, he titled his collections with the theatricality of Ziegfeld—Zig-Zag (1948), Oblique (1950), Arrow (1956), Libre (1957), to name four—and in so doing immortalized his changing vision, his lines, even as he angered women tired of being turned into Tulips (1953). It's hard to believe that Dior's classic A-line dates merely to 1955. Today it seems the first letter of fashion, a perfect symbol of haute couture: three lines that suggest the Eiffel Tower that stands for Paris.

LINE

GIANNI VERSACE ATELIER, 1994–1995: EVENING ENSEMBLE IN SILK TAFFETA, TOPSTITCHED TO SUGGEST BONING.

W e live in clothes the way we live in rooms, hoping for security, delight, and design that will not age overnight. Couturiers understand this intimacy. No matter how big the company (at its peak, Worth employed 1,200 workers), the couturier's establishment is referred to as a House.

GIVENCHY, 1991: A GOWN MODELED IN THE DESIGNER'S HOME.

Focusing on a wreath of laurel,

Givenchy's bronze shows us

line as wisdom: the full circle.

Looking beyond both women,

we see line as fire: the gilded

arabesque. And for simplicity,

let your eye fall upon the folds

of the sculpted cloth ⌒ which

seem to counsel that sumptuous

persimmon skirt, seem to say

"follow me." Couturiers who

don't know history, art, and

architecture at the beginning of

their careers? They learn.

GIVENCHY, 1991: ORGANZA BODICE PETALED WITH
MOTHER-OF-PEARL SEQUINS AND VARIOUS BRILLIANTS
ATOP A POUF OF APRICOT SILK TAFFETA.

CLAUDE MONTANA FOR LANVIN,
1990: JACKET IN RUSSIAN
OLIVE SATIN (LEFT).
BALMAIN, 1989: HIGH-
NECKED, LONG-SLEEVED
VELVET JACKET WITH
EMBROIDERED BORDER
(FACING PAGE).

Consummate finish is a hallmark of haute couture. The
creamy curve of Montana's bolero, its effortlessly
turned edge and authoritative collar points,
carry the eye in a lyrelike loop ⏑ Orpheus
ascending. Balmain's border relies on
massed extravagance; its music is
ceremonial ⏑ the trumpet fanfare
with a hint of war.

Line is not simply outline, an exclamation from the drafts- man's pen; it can also be a com- plex configuration that leads the eye to epiphany. Here, Gérard Pipart sets up a powerful counterpoint between the climbing calm of an embroidered black velvet column and the bold splash of a red silk overskirt. All points meet just under the bosom, where that happy bow has landed like a butterfly, rhyming with the décolletage above it. Within its snug high waistband, the dress gathers a bouquet of troubador allusions, and offers historical homage to that queen of the bust—the Minoan goddess.

GÉRARD PIPART FOR NINA RICCI, 1989: A STRAPLESS SHEATH OF EMBROIDERED ROSES ON BLACK VELVET, SKIRTED IN RED THAI SILK.

GIVENCHY, 1992: STRAPLESS POLKA-
DOT GOWN WITH POUF PEPLUM IN
REVERSE POLKA DOTS.

*W*hen a designer's ideas are pirated, it is line that constitutes the most egregious steal. After all, fabrication is not sacrosanct, and details can be finessed. No, poachers go for silhouette, for shape, which is why sketching was so long verboten at shows. Alas, nothing can be done about a photographic memory, mental notes like: ballerina peplum, float of skirt, deep folds caught up and flowering at the heart.

Each couturier brings different gifts to the art, and each approaches design uniquely. Some, like painters, make their breakthrough on the blank page, pencil sketching their silhouettes in two dimensions. Others, like sculptors, work tactilely, draping and shaping material on a model, letting the fabric have a voice, giving bias a bias. What all approaches have in common is the search for an organizing principle, a linear rationale. In Scaasi's gown all lines lead to the solar plexus, where a knot of high priestess antiquity, and high emotion, has been placed like an oracle. Galanos shows us a shifting sand of shirred lines, unified by two bolts from the blue.

SCAASI, 1989: PEARLED AND SEQUINED WHITE CHIFFON GOWN KNOTTED UNDER THE BUST (LEFT). GALANOS, 1984: GOWN WITH RIBBONS AND GATHERS WORKED ON THE BIAS (FACING PAGE).

The princess line. It sounds like a cruise ship and in fact it was introduced in the 1860s, when women did sail along in floor-length gowns with skirts that trailed like wakes. The princess line is distinguished by its lack of a horizontal waist seam; instead, the silhouette is conceived vertically, with two longitudinal seams traveling over the bust from shoulder to hem, behaving like discreet darts, answering feminine curves with utmost subtlety. The line is also known as fourreau or sheath, but princess better suggests its sense of court decorum—a sweet uprightness that both Venet and Givenchy have honored in these strapless gowns.

PHILIPPE VENET, 1990: STRAP-LESS AND APPLIQUÉD PRINCESS-SEAMED GOWN (BELOW). GIVENCHY, 1990: EMBROIDERED GOWN IN PINK GAZAR WITH DANCING SKIRT (FACING PAGE).

S*callops and scales and wave upon wave upon wave, and glittering verticals, reminiscent of fin de siècle corsetting, nod to the whalebone that came from the sea that shaped the ladies. Valentino's melee of curves and perpendiculars points to where the surf meets the sand and Venus emerges.*

VALENTINO, 1990: TIERED COLUMN OF LEMON
CHIFFON PIN PLEATS UNDER SCALLOPED TUNIC
RIBBONED IN DIAMANTÉ.

Wearing its wingspan like an F-16, remembering the runway in parallel seams, looking almost as if the shadows had been sewn in and the sunlight told where to pose ⁓ Venet's kimono coat is a model of linear control and aerodynamic elegance. Origami that flies and enfolds.

PHILIPPE VENET, 1994–
1995: DOUBLE-
FACED CASHMERE
KIMONO-CUT COAT.

Can an elaborate design be the setting for

one great line? Of course it can. Like a

sonnet that rounds to a closing couplet,

this gown of big and small circles contains

its own suggestive closure: a row of diamond-

ite buttons that grow gradually smaller as they

approach the waist, each diminishing sphere

an increasingly private punctuation.

GALANOS, 1991: TUNIC-TOPPED
CREPE EVENING DRESS WITH A
MINIFISHTAIL IN BACK OVER
A LONG, NARROW, SLIT SKIRT.

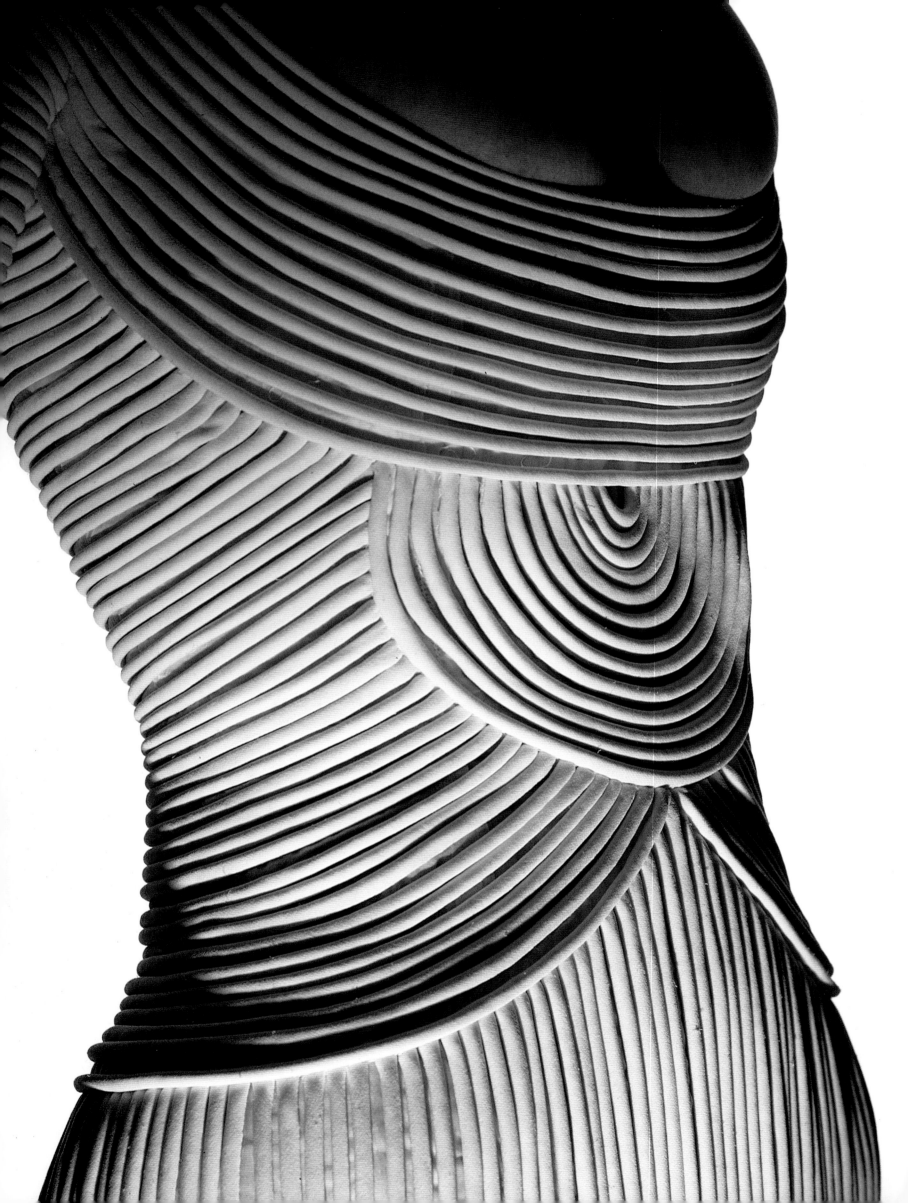

Texture is not just the physical properties of soft and hard, coarse and fine, sheer and plush. In haute couture, texture is the beginning, a dress's "Once upon a time." The word primarily means the process or art of weaving, but it grows out of the word text, *which the Oxford English Dictionary defines as "style, tissue of a literary work." Deep in human history, the acts of telling a story and of weaving a fabric are one. The Bible, of course, makes this point repeatedly, with its linen scrolls and Veronica's veils, and perhaps most profoundly in the story of Moses, whose rough scrap of swaddling is later evidence of his Hebrew birth, telling the tale through woof and warp. Material comes off the loom complete with its own genre: canvas is a Homeric epic, painted silk a haiku, thick velvet a passion play, stretch knit a limerick. Sometimes, to tell a very specific story, designers will come up with their own "material" (as Valentino has here), and then the result is a soliloquy worthy of Shakespeare.*

VALENTINO, 1993: WHITE SILK SATIN SPAGHETTI-STRING EVENING DRESS WITH PLISSÉ CHIFFON UNDERSKIRT.

GIVENCHY, 1991:
SCARLET SILK
JUMPSUIT TOPPED
WITH A FUR-CUFFED
WOOLEN OPERA COAT.

Silk, lambswool, fur. Though the weave and the working are subject to technology's innovations, these centuries-old textures have changed little over time. Constancy is a form of luxury. Change often equals loss. This particular combination ⌒ soft on soft on soft ⌒ was available before the Fall.

UNGARO, 1994–1995: BLACK
VELVET DRESS EMBROIDERED
WITH SILK THREAD ROSES; WHITE
SILK RUFFLE OVER A BLACK
TULLE RUFFLE. DETAIL OF
CHIFFON SLEEVE EMBROIDERED
WITH JET (OVERLEAF).

You can pleat a ruffle, gather a ruffle, even crimp wrinkles into a ruffle. Born of abundance, distant daughter to the neck ruff, sister to froth, foam, and tropical fish fins, the ruffle is frivolous and fantastique. Except for Flamenco, where mucho ruffles dance with mortality, ruffle upon ruffle is sure fashion disaster⌣unless a master proportions the pinch!

The ribbon is innocent.

Or it is not. It is the shepherdess's ornament, the not-so-coy mistress's token of esteem. Pastel, it decorates baby clothes and girls' smocking; black, it is fastened around the neck of nude Olympias. Ribbon is witty. Woven through wool or netting it creates a texture of total surprise. Here, Lagerfeld's yellow ribbon sprigging suggests the straw and the stablemaid—Coco Chanel's love of horses and the fresh outlines of her famous suit.

Brocade is a fairy tale. Its figures are woven into a spellbound cloth, a story told over and over, yard by yard, in Rumpelstiltskin gold (or silver) threads. The Jacquard loom, invented in the early 1800s, made this magic possible. Ever since, brocade has been associated with enchanted evenings.

VERA WANG, 1991: EVENING DRESS OF SILVER-AND-GOLD BROCADE, DENSELY CUFFED WITH SILVER-AND-GOLD BEADING.

A wrinkle in time⁓this figure of speech implies a momentary warp, a glimpse into infinity. In fact, Valentino's minutely draped bodice might be the fabled ocean that lay at earth's center. Suggesting the kind of compression that creates diamonds, these strata of silk are achieved with fingers and thread, a technique brought to a pitch of perfection by the legendary couturier Madame Grès. Her interest was in antiquity⁓Delphic folds and the wise wind's fluting. How is such delicacy captured? Not, as in quilting, from the top, but underneath, one swift invisible stitch at a time.

Valentino, 1989: Brown chiffon bodice fitted amid deeply embroidered waistline and sleeves (facing page). Valentino, 1990: Lamé and quilted-satin short coat (right).

"... Close the serpent sly, Insinuating," writes John Milton in Book IV of Paradise Lost. This gown concurs, though not in words, insinuating that temptation is twined into every great design. And calculation. For despite the latest technology, sequin work such as this cannot be bought by the yard. Each slim disc must be sewn on by hand, stitch by single stitch, and placed according to a couturier's specific pattern. A time-consuming process that is mastered by few, the result is a gleaming second skin ⁓or in this case, snakeskin⁓ a vision of Eve deceived; of woman at the moment of knowledge; of Paradise, potentially, found.

ERIK MORTENSEN FOR BALMAIN, 1989: GOWN OF GOLD
AND BLACK SEQUINS ON TULLE.

Some materials have light woven in: velvet traps shadows in its nap, silk wears sheen like a well-groomed cat. The attraction of oddball textures such as patent leather and vinyl are the liquid flash, the splash of color. Sequins are more like spotlights banked to illuminate clean curves, O's of opalescence that articulate the figure's syllables. Norell's sequined sheath makes live theater of the body in motion, a thousand tiny gels fixed on every move, the heroine's mood in glittering flux.

Norell, late 1960s: Sequined slip-dress.

It has been deemed the most flattering fabric in the world, and though its truest calling may be to grace royalty in red, velvet has served haute couture from the start. The name comes from the Latin vellus, for "fleece" or "tufted hair," a nod to its plush pillowiness, its neat nape. Velvet has its finest hour when made from silk and cut on the bias, coating curves like glycerine. But it is black velvet that rules the imagination ⁓ unfailingly grave as collar or cuff, operetta chic as party dress.

YVES SAINT LAURENT, 1994–1995: BLACK VELVET AND TULLE EVENING DRESS.

DRAPE &
PLEAT

Touch is the first test of a designer's desire to know a fabric better. Just as "nose" is the first key to a wine's character, its fragrant introduction to the air, "hand" is the term for a material's sass and spring, its singular feel between palm and fingers. Next comes the urge to unfurl the bolt and drape a path of fabric across the body, noting how it flows, crumples, and catches light. Great satins, velvets, and chiffons may want nothing more from life. Look at Renaissance angels, for instance, masters of the falling fold, in which the mysteries of grace correspond to the geometries of gravity. They make the equation that drape is gesture, reminding us it is the heavenly hem's meeting with the earth that creates this dialogue of light and shadow. Greece and Rome are home to the pleat. Even classical columns wear them. Without plenty, neither drape nor pleat is possible—each technique requires triple the length of material normally needed. Is it any surprise then, that the robe, the cape, the chiton is the fashion worn by our oracles, our winged wise?

CHRISTIAN LACROIX, 1994–1995:
APPLE GREEN SATIN SKIRT.

The extra yardage required for a draped design automatically means disobedience ⁓ unexpected escapes and escapades. This is why pleats are often top- or edge-stitched, why gathers are tacked in place. Secured simply at shoulder and hip, this study in loose line is also a performance: the mercurial dance of atmosphere; Ariel's abandon.

GIVENCHY, 1990: RED GOWN OF DRAPED AND SWATHED SILK, WITH CAPE SLEEVES.

R enowned for

the creamy contours

he coaxed from duchess

satin, Cristóbal Balenciaga

set the standard for shapes that

intuit a material's mood. He

sculpted archetypes with a butter

knife. When Balenciaga closed his

house in 1968, many of his work-

people and clientele went over to

Givenchy, who was mentored by

the master. White as a wingspan,

inching glacially, Givenchy's bod-

ice celebrates the classical touch.

GIVENCHY, 1989: OFF-WHITE SATIN STRAPLESS GOWN.

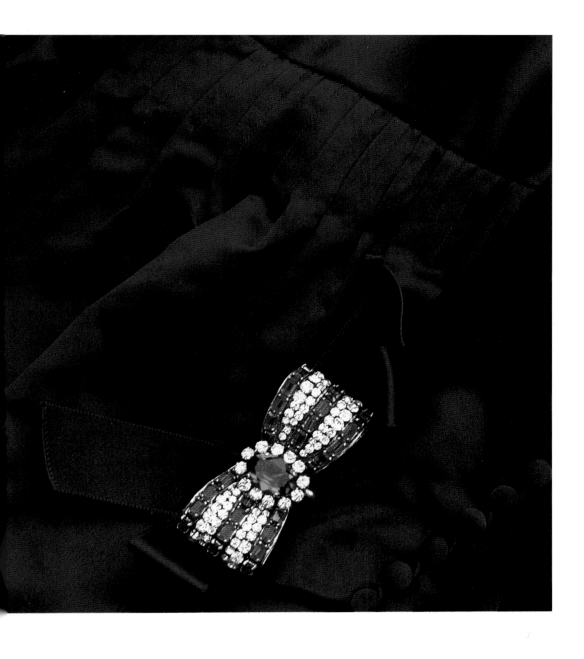

KARL LAGERFELD FOR
CHANEL, 1994–1995:
BLACK SATIN DRESS
WITH SHIRTWAIST LINE
AND TOPSTITCHED
KNIFE PLEATS.

Stitching pleats, box pleats, knife pleats,

cartridge pleats, godets in slashes⁓each

pleat has its own personality. But all line

up in rows like soldiers (hence the knives

and cartridges and slashes), which is

perhaps why Lagerfeld has added a

patriotic pin to this black satin dress.

An evening coat worn like a dressing gown ⁓ tossed on, slippage built in, billowing down the hallway like a second temperament. Too much decorum is stifling. A little grand déshabillé can let air into a garment grown tense and too predictable.

*T*ransformations — caterpillar to butterfly, duckling to swan, Miss to Mrs. — are traditionally attended by the hush and pageant of fabric. In the Wendy Hiller — Leslie Howard film Pygmalion, *the long reach down for her satin skirts punctuates Eliza's triumph at the ball: a prince waits as she prepares to take a step. In Billy Wilder's movie* Sabrina, *Audrey Hepburn's debut at the Larrabee fête takes place in a Paris original "with yards of skirt, and way off the shoulder." And of course, centuries of Cinderella would be moot without a gossamer gown to sweep in the new. The big dress is everything. It opens space for the blossoming — creating room around the wearer, and filling that room with authenticating aura. Looking back to the start of his career, Valentino tells of his shock and delight upon seeing a Dior gown that took 26 yards of taffeta, 50 yards of trim edging neckline and hem. Vive la volume! If it weren't for these swirls and swaths and sails, we would lose the singlemost feminine formality in Western history: a woman's ushering of her ballgown skirt.*

VALENTINO, 1992: BLACK SILK VELVET AND TULLE EVENING DRESS WITH WHITE SILK SATIN RIBBON APPLICATION.

The sensual appeal of chiffon ⁓ its sheer lightness ⁓ is only magnified when used voluminously. Then it takes on the oxymoron of heavy lightness, of body. Lagerfeld calls the color of this gown cuisse de nymphe émue, or "maiden's blush," and indeed it does play about the shoulder and thigh like putti with too knowing a touch.

KARL LAGERFELD FOR CHANEL, 1990: PALE PINK CHIFFON GOWN LOOPED HIGH ON THE LEGS AND LOW AT THE BUST.

*Though the wearer be silent,
the dress is fortissimo.
Yves Saint Laurent turns
up the volume not only
with free-flowing bolts of
silk bannered from the
neckline, but through
purity of form. This gown
reads like a proclamation,
a two-part theorem on the
essential simplicity of
grandeur, a geometric
proof in which rectangles
and triangles speak for
the throat.*

YVES SAINT LAURENT, 1989: PURPLE SATIN
CHIFFON WITH RED CAPE AND COPPER SCARF.

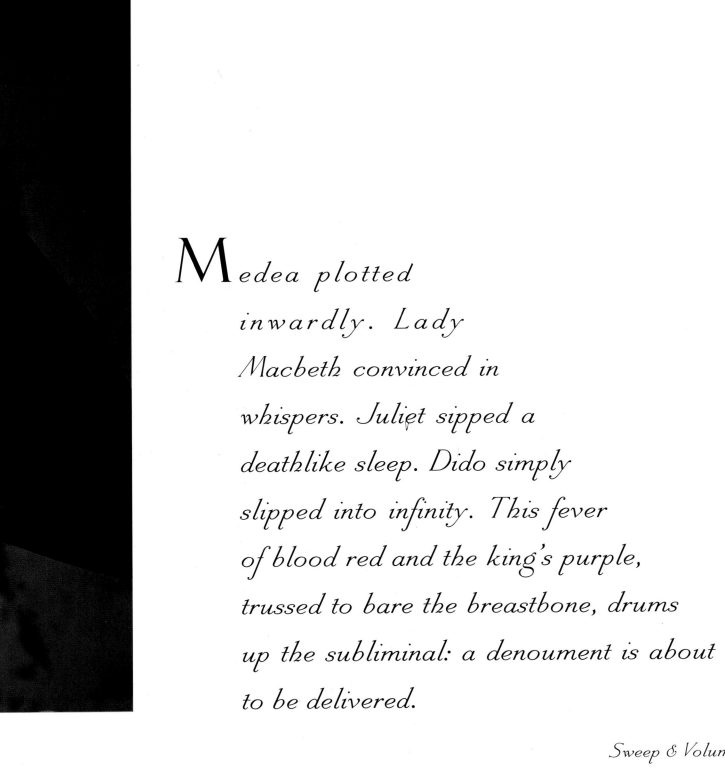

Medea plotted
inwardly. Lady
Macbeth convinced in
whispers. Juliet sipped a
deathlike sleep. Dido simply
slipped into infinity. This fever
of blood red and the king's purple,
trussed to bare the breastbone, drums
up the subliminal: a denoument is about
to be delivered.

GIANFRANCO FERRÉ FOR DIOR, 1989: CHIFFON BALL GOWN WITH FLOWER-CLUSTER BODICE.

A design dictum goes, "Two is better than one, if one is better than none." A comment in praise of quality first, it's also a tactful bit of caution for those not yet ready to be lavish. Excess can be full of glee, as we know from the Rococo; it can be a liberation, as the Romantics showed. But it requires knowledge. Ferré sees through a garden darkly: more is more.

John Anthony, 1991: Ballgown
in electric blue satin with deep
collar of white organza.

Bertha is the name for this capelike collar,
traditionally made of lace. It dates to the mid-
nineteenth century and conjures up spinsters in
sitting rooms, shoulders curved like cameos. In
white organza, however, the bertha should be
renamed. For the belle of the ball, or the bride.

Bustles

of the late nineteenth century were known
as "dress improvers," and in fact they did offer an
ideal landscape for the decorative upsweep of over-
skirts. Yves Saint Laurent acknowledges history with a
behemothic bow, while also employing one of the
most effective design tactics: skyscraper scale
where you least expect it.

Whether it be marquisette or matelassé or moiré or mousseline ⁓ and those are just the M's ⁓ silk is haute couture's thread of choice. A natural wonder of the world, silk originated in China, a luxury spun by the grub of the silk-worm moth. Is it farfetched to name the first couturier Bombyx mori? After all, each silk creation is just another step of the metamorphosis that begins in that cocoon.

UNGARO, 1989: SILK TAFFETA GOWN
(FACING PAGE). ADOLFO, 1991:
MOUSSELINE CAFTAN (BELOW).
SCASSI, 1991: CHIFFON EVENING
DRESS (OVERLEAF).

I**t is not exactly scientific, but how air mixes with material is a couture consideration. Designers have strategies for inflecting the ineffable, focusing the featherweight. Be it scaffoldings of tulle or sheer organza, or a swathed waist, as here, the leap of the skirt is lovely, but not if it continually goes too high.**

LOUIS FÉRAUD, 1990: PLEATED MELON *MOUSSELINE* GOWN WITH JEWELED LAPEL.

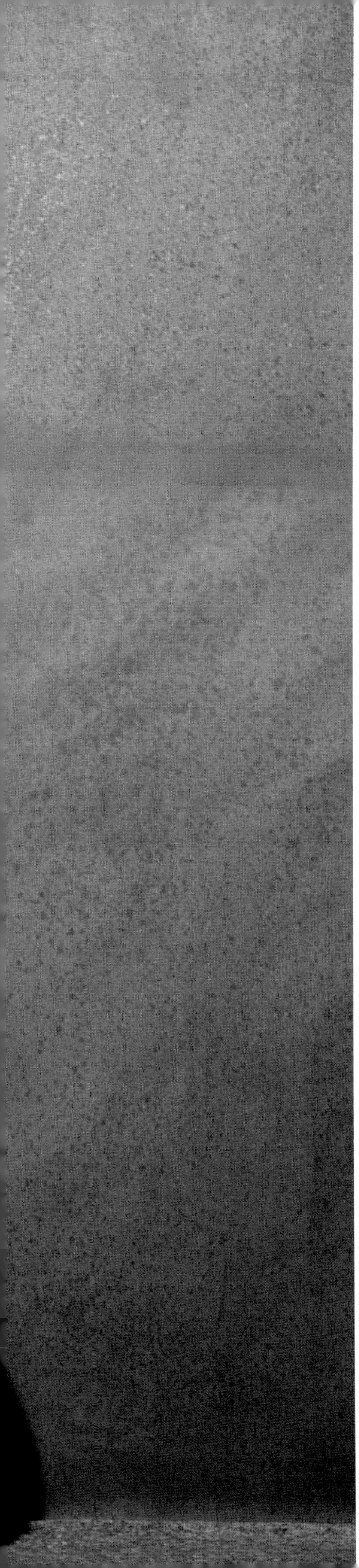

I*t is women who grace the*

ship's prow, women for whom

hurricanes are named. Female

as force of nature is the un-

spoken assumption of this

silvered spinnaker of a

cape. When not catching a

city breeze, this stiff satin

creates its own floating

wake in a woman's walk.

CLAUDE MONTANA FOR LANVIN, 1990:
LAVENDER AND SILVER SATIN CAPE
OVER GLITTERING MINIDRESS.

As curtains, they are called Austrians, and the Old World formality of such exaggerated upsweep has swagged many a mansion view. Americans, in their New World buoyancy, call them "balloon shades." In a gown that employs the same tiered technique, Ferré offers a window on both worlds: cozy materialism and pockets of air.

GIANFRANCO FERRÉ FOR CHRISTIAN DIOR, 1992:
STRAPLESS, TWO-TIERED SILK BALL GOWN
(RIGHT). CHRISTIAN LACROIX, 1992:
MULTILAYERED PARTY DRESS (OVERLEAF).

ORNAMENT

When he established his fashion house in 1858, Charles Frederick Worth became the first father of Paris haute couture. His surname symbolized something of what his customers were buying, for it was the Second Empire, an era of new wealth and decorative display, and Worth dressed its richest women. Who would have guessed his early background in the London drapery-wares firm of Swan and Edgar, with its heavy trims and fringes, tassels and laces, would lend itself so well to the grand monde. Fashioning her green velvet curtains into a dress à la mode, Scarlett O'Hara paid pure if unintentional homage to Worth, who turned out a well-upholstered, opulently appointed mansion of a woman (in the late 1800s, when skirts were drawn up onto the hips, the look was called style tapissier, "upholsterer style"). As time ran out on the hourglass shape, ornamentation was no longer layered in bolts and handfuls upon an unchanging form, but became modern⁓ an expression of wit or sly social commentary or, as in the dress on this page, voluptuous restraint.

GALANOS, 1994: DOUBLE-LAYERED, BIAS-CUT PALE PINK SILK SATIN GOWN WITH BRA TOP MADE WITH CRYSTALS AND PALE PINK CAVIAR BEADS.

Art, nature, literature, the past—the designer's search for inspiration never ends. Magic, however, can lurk surprisingly close to home, in the workshops of artisans who create new enchantments. It has been said that haute couture lives in Paris because Paris itself is home to incomparable ribbon and button makers, bead and embroidery houses. A conjuring of crown jewels; Daphne springing into flower: such notions first peeked from a little local cardboard box.

KARL LAGERFELD FOR CHANEL, 1989: RUBY RED CHIFFON GOWN WITH RHINESTONE NECKLACE (ABOVE). VALENTINO, 1989: DRAPED BODICE WITH MANTLE OF BEADED CHIFFON FLOWERS (FACING PAGE).

One of France's great aesthetes was an English creation: novelist Nancy Mitford's unforgettable character Charles-Edouard de Valhubert. "Nature I hate," was one of his singular assessments — a dig at the English and a cry for cultivation. Pastoral perfection wasn't nearly enough. If it were, for instance, this white gown would need no embellishment, for it is cool perfection already, fitting the model's peaks and valleys without a wrinkle, a lovely flutter at the bust. But is the dress happy in its virgin state? The couturier heeds its silent, siren song, and with crystal beads and silver, nets a fantastic simplicity: a mermaid from Crete.

CLAUDE MONTANA FOR LANVIN, 1990:
CREPE SHEATH WITH CRYSTAL FISHNET.

Lorelei Lee may have banked on her bosom (while preferring diamonds), and men used to hide money in their shirts, but in the terms of antiquity the bust was the seat of thought and feeling—the soul sculpted in marble. Ferré's glittering and definitive bodice catches all the connotations: the goddess and the golddigger and the goods.

KARL LAGERFELD FOR
CHANEL, 1989: FITTED,
SLIPPER-SATIN DINNER
SUIT, DEEPLY BEADED
AND EMBROIDERED.

E*laborate needlework wants
time and space. It must be
thoroughly conceived from the
start and, so that the embroiderer
can work on flat surfaces, completed
before the dress is constructed. Lagerfeld's
panels of Baroque banners and bows tell an
ebullient truth: only imperial courts ⁓ and
couturiers ⁓ have the means for such fancy.*

Before he opened his own house,
Worth learned the dressmaking trade at Gagelin
and Opigez in the rue Richelieu. It was a company that
specialized in "confections," that is, cloaks, shawls,
and mantles. In its detail and sweep, Lacroix's
lavender mantle is itself a confection
worthy of Worth.

T*ulle originated in the eighteenth century in a French town of the same name. This mighty mesh of hexagons, beloved by the ballet, offers the couturier an airy canvas upon which sequins, beads, and dewdrops can be secured in dancing patterns, through which ribbons and feathers can be woven, and secret details seen, discreetly.*

GIVENCHY, 1991: BLACK TULLE GOWN STRAPPED AND BOWED IN BLACK VELVET, AND SPRINKLED WITH BLACK PAILLETTES.

Of all the needles in the couturier trade, none is as lithe or blithe as the beading needle. Long as a ring finger, hair-fine, this supple piece of steel with the squint eye skims and sways about the surface of its favorite fabrics ⌒ silk, tulle, net, and lace ⌒ the world's tiniest magic wand. Nothing is impossible for the accomplished embroiderer, a fairy godmother granting the wishes of her designer.

SCHERRER, 1990: FLORAL BEADED TULLE TEE, WITH CREPE JACKET.

$\mathcal{S}$equin

comes from the Italian

zecchino — a Venetian gold

coin — so perhaps it's no surprise

that the Italian Elsa Schiaparelli

experimented early with these slips of

light. Geoffrey Beene, who names the

daring and playful artist as a mentor,

takes the sequin still further into

foreign territory, minting a

bodice of racy, struc-

tural luxe.

GEOFFREY BEENE, 1991:
ORANGE SATIN BALL GOWN WITH
A SEQUIN-PAVÉD HALTER TOP AND
BEAD-ENCRUSTED BOLERO.

Before it became the word
for caviar-small glass and steel
spheres, bead had a hallowed
meaning: prayer. To "tell beads"
(think rosary!) was to count prayers.
It's a visceral connection: beading requires
a bowed concentration, an intimate rhythm,
a repetition felt in the fingers and palm, and a
vision not just beyond the moment, but Beyond.

As each bead and appliqué is stitched in place, the cloth grows heavy. Except in the sheerest concoctions, the fabric has been prepared for such stress with a facing of linen or silk (in Asia, embroidery is often backed with paper), which is why it makes sense for a design's ornamentation to become, as in these two creations, both architectural underpinning and pinnacle.

ERIK MORTENSEN FOR BALMAIN, 1990: GOLD T-STRAP GOWN (FACING PAGE). GUY LAROCHE, 1989: CHIFFON GOWN EMBROIDERED WITH SILVER THREAD.

Oh Rose, thou art pink! And made of satin or velvet or felt or even, as here, of matching organza. Thou art tea rose, beach rose, sweetheart rose, or, as here, rose a size we've never seen before. The couturier knows two perfect ornaments: the bow and the rose. Chances are, the rose came first.

VALENTINO, 1990: TIERED TOP WITH APPLIQUÉ FLOWERS (ABOVE). GÉRARD PIPART FOR NINA RICCI, 1990: BLUSH-COLOR ORGANZA (FACING PAGE).

Fashion has always swung between escalating extravagance and corrective austerity, a cycle tied to kings and courts, to first ladies and the ticker-tape parade. Embroidery, passementerie, and the art of appliqué reflect a royal past in which coils of gold and silver measured status, "decoration" carried a connotation of loyalty, service, and honor; and the deeply wrought and glittering surface was an aesthetic armor against time and fate's decrees.

GIVENCHY, 1989: BLUE SATIN DRESS EMBELLISHED WITH GOLDEN PEARLS (BELOW). KARL LAGERFELD FOR CHANEL, 1989: WHITE SATIN JACKET COVERED WITH GOLD PASSEMENTERIE (FACING PAGE).

Woe to that artist who loses a sense of play. Dallies, romps, and frolics are a form of experiment, a pushing of perception and craft that can lead to exhilarating images or technical breakthroughs or funny flops or simply a better understanding of why the boundaries exist where they do. How do couturiers play? With puns (Schiaparelli's shoe hat) and juxtapositions (Beene's sequined football jersey), overstatement (Lacroix's Belle Epoque poufs) and understatement (Balenciaga's Amphora Line), allusions (Dior's Degas bodice) and delusions (Lagerfeld's tweed hotpants). Haute couture is a history of visions ⁓ creations that comment on female sexuality and psyche, woman's place in the household and in the culture. As with the metaphysical poets, metaphor is the couturier's trick of choice: she is animal, vegetable, mineral. Here, she is a bridal bouquet. Is it any surprise that in 1995 one of the world's top fashion models dated one of the world's top magicians? From flat cloth the couturier conjures one shapely illusion after another ⁓ a collection of new possibilities.

GIVENCHY, 1991: WHITE ORGANZA SHEATH COVERED WITH SPRAYS OF LILY OF THE VALLEY AND BOWED WITH WHITE ORGANZA.

Woman as objet d'art. In feminist terms that means woman objectified ⁓ Galatea in her gown of marble. In this case, however, it is clearly the suit that's the objet. Givenchy's exercise in trompe l'oeil is a test of texture and tone and the needle's precision. She, meanwhile, is the bird in the gilded age.

There are some who say that there's
nothing new under the sun. And true, icons of the past
— royalty, film stars, literary figures — have often provided designers with a reference point and a starting point.
In which case, who better to return to than Ra? Or is it
Cleopatra? Or maybe it's the druid queen Norma,
preparing to worship the moon.

Film noir—a glare, a shadow,

a city street, no fingerprints!

Science fiction—the Invisible

Woman on a Parisian prowl.

Fairy tale—the clock strikes

twelve and Cinderella's dress

heads home without her. A little

tulle, a little velvet, some sequins

and thread: Mystery.

GIVENCHY, 1994–1995:
BLACK TULLE EVENING
DRESS WITH GRADUATED
SEQUINS AND TWO
VELVET BOWS.

Is it Don Juan's little black book? The eternal woman inside? The elaborate appliqué on this bustier dress is not only a virtuoso performance in stiff symmetry, it recalls the gold embossing of a fine leatherbound volume, which itself opens up a series of associations: wealth, aristocracy, family tree, history. This contemporary donna wears the stamp of centuries.

GUY LAROCHE, 1989: A BELL-SHAPED BUSTIER CUT LONG, AND DENSELY DECORATED WITH GOLD APPLIQUÉ AND EMBROIDERY.

For those who wonder how

fashion speaks, what

messages are encoded in its

techniques, this Galanos gown is

a perfect place to play hide and seek.

At first glance that white tulle ruffle

performs the part of boa, or "fascinator," as

the Victorians called them for the way they

framed the face with motion. And yet this energetic

tumble points further back, to Italy's Pierrots and

bouncing acrobats. It's not a boa but a huge commedia

dell'arte ruff, and she the star coquette.

The Temple of Wisdom, the Queen of the Night. The pursuit of the universe is not beyond the couturier, but the touch must be light ⌣ a flight. What better model than Mozart's Magic Flute, where intellect comes dressed in noble tunics, and the ancient opposition of dark and light finds harmony in the heroine's breast: the sun, heart-high at midnight.

The body seen as a strange continent: a fantasy island where décolletage forms an exotic inlet, and velvet shimmers like mother-of-pearl, and silk skirts wear a seashell ruffle, an anemone's air. Lacroix's undine is part Folies-Bergère, part water ballet. But is this a Paleozoic landscape or the far, far future?

 ougainvillea was the inspiration for this masterpiece, its thousands of sequins and semiprecious stones stitched one at a time and taking over 900 hours of work. In a breeze, the raised petals nod slightly, as if remembering that first garden where, with eyes newly opened, a newly unhappy couple found a fig tree, "And with what skill they had together sewed."

YVES SAINT LAURENT, 1989: CAPE EMBROIDERED
BY M. LESAGE.

DRAMA

*E*ver since Worth dressed Sarah Bernhardt and Eleonora Duse, aristocrats of the stage have shared the top of the couture client list with royalty. Divas and primas and starlets are treasured customers, and since the beginning, who-dressed-who has been part of the social code. For example, think Margot Fonteyn and you think Dior; Audrey Hepburn, Givenchy; Jeanne Moreau, Cardin. Constantly photographed, these artists launch trends as readily as the latest princess or president's wife. In fact, couturiers have frequently designed specifically for the theater, a world not unlike their own, as anyone who has seen a fashion show knows. Carefully planned in tempo, momentum, and dramatic impact, the "collections," which were first shown in private Paris salons to women in white gloves, are today a part of the contemporary landscape — a spectator sport seen on TV. The ultimate drama, of course, is the dress itself. The truth is, no matter how life evolves, there will always be moments when making an entrance is all.

Ungaro, 1989: Scarlet silk satin gown.

CHRISTIAN LACROIX,
1994–1995: RED
SATIN PARTY DRESS.

To put on the finished
work of a couturier is one of
life's great luxuries. Fittings, like re-
hearsals, have led to the awaited moment,
akin to an opening night. It must be perfect.
The true connoisseur, however, appreciates the
inside as much as the effect. Understanding how it
happened ⌒ technique! ⌒ is an interior drama unto itself.

T*he*

rose is a symbol of love. Each color

has meaning, emotion shading from purity to pas-

sion. The red, red rose is the heart of romance litera-

ture, the burning cheek of the mistress. And the silver rose?

A communiqué, a highly formal, eighteenth-century decla-

ration of intent. Ungaro's *gown is a* Rosenkavalier *waltz,*

a Perrault fairy tale, a topiary garden stocked with

roses of sterling descent.

UNGARO, 1990: POUF JACKET OF SILVER
AND GOLD LAMÉ WITH AN OVERSKIRT OF
MOSS GREEN FLEATED SILK.

As much as cut and cloth, skin figures in the couturier's vision. How much to show and where to show it is determined not only by the design in mind, but by the character of the woman inside the design. Is it a beautiful bosom? Is the posture appropriate? Can she carry it off? Montana's plunge to the waist calls for nerves of steel, a collaborative attack on the status quo.

CLAUDE MONTANA FOR LANVIN,
1990: STEEL GRAY ORGANZA
BENEATH A KNIT BODICE THAT
GLISTENS WITH METAL BEADS.

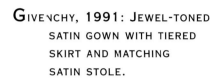

GIVENCHY, 1991: JEWEL-TONED
SATIN GOWN WITH TIERED
SKIRT AND MATCHING
SATIN STOLE.

The great operatic entrances happen on stairways.

At the ballet, the maiden usually comes to us

under a veil, or attended by coryphées. But

what of the great exits? Nothing quits a room

like a scarf or stole. Above all, a satin stole,

which knights the shoulders with dignity, and

a flashing finish.

KAFL LAGERFELD
FOR CHANEL, 1990:
PERSIMMON SATIN
REDINGOTE THAT
PARTS ON BOOTS
AND MINIDRESS.

This red redingote is a double whammy.

Both the word and the shape came to France from the

English "riding coat," an equestrian silhouette that evolved into

a lady's long outer garment in the nineteenth century. The scar-

let, or "pink," of the fox hunt rides along as a second associa-

tion. And once Lagerfeld throws in those thigh-high

boots ⁓ military majesty at full gallop.

Ungaro,
1994–1995:
EMBROIDERED
SATIN WEDDING
DRESS IN PALE
GREEN, GOLD,
AND PINK, WITH
PINK LACE-
EMBROIDERED
OVERSKIRT.
FAN-PLEATED
ELIZABETHAN
COLLAR (OVERLEAF).

Just as so many stories end
with a wedding, the haute couture
collection has traditionally ended with
a wedding dress. Of all the events in a
woman's life, the wedding is the most planned,
choreographed, and stage-managed, and the dress is
a queen-for-a-day affair. Ungaro's infanta-inspired bridal
gown acknowledges the royal connotations of marriage—
the drawing up of a new, small, social institution—each
stitch sanctioning that domain of two.

ADOLFO SARDIÑA *(b. 1930) was born in Havana, Cuba, and emigrated to New York City in 1948. Although his adolescent ambition was to design dresses, he began his career making hats, first as an apprentice milliner at Bergdorf Goodman, and then as Adolfo of Emme. In 1958 he went to Paris and worked for four years in Balenciaga's hat salon. He returned to New York in 1962 and opened his own millinery salon. Adolfo inched into dressmaking—which he had learned in the 1950s from Ana Maria Borrero, a Cuban designer who had studied with Poiret and Patou— when clients began asking about the dresses he made for models to wear with his hats. The classic Adolfo dress or suit is a supple knit tailored along clean, rather conservative lines. For women in power positions it is often the suit of choice.*

JOHN ANTHONY *(b. 1942) was born in New York City, the son of an Italian-American sculptor. While attending the High School of Industrial Arts, he was awarded a scholarship to the Accademia d'Arte in Rome. After spending several years in Italy, he returned to New York to continue study at the Fashion Institute of Technology. Anthony's own firm emerged in the 1970s, and his meticulously crafted collections have earned him a reputation as fashion's minimalist.*

CRISTÓBAL BALENCIAGA *(1895–1972) was a natural. The oft-repeated story is that of a boy who told a wealthy woman he could copy her couture suit in one night—and did. This woman became Balenciaga's patron, helping the self-taught young man set up his first tailoring shops in Spain. When he opened his house in Paris in 1937, it was the beginning of three decades in which he was the undisputed high priest of fashion. And around him there was a hush. Balenciaga did not care for press or publicity; the international royalty he dressed were word enough. And a Balenciaga was not for Everywoman—it took a*

strong character, a beautiful posture, to wear these creations of almost preternatural perfection. Indeed, he liked to work in fabrics of strong character as well: wools, taffetas, silk gazar. Balenciaga closed his house in 1968, a sobering moment in fashion history.

The house of PIERRE BALMAIN *(1914–1982) opened in 1945, just two years before the house of Dior. Both men had come of age designing for Lucien Lelong, working together in such close collaboration that they would joke about not knowing who designed what. Balmain was born in Saint-Jean-de-Maurienne, France, to a family in the drapery business. He studied architecture, but left school to apprentice with Captain Molyneux. Once on his own, the Balmain label came to signify design that was feminine and flirtatious, wearing an air of classical chic. A Balmain evening gown was considered the ultimate in sophisticated expression.* ERIK MORTENSEN *(b. 1926) came to Balmain in 1948. Born in the north of Denmark, he studied with Holger Blum, Copenhagen's premier couturier. In 1950 Mortensen became Balmain's right-hand man, and upon Balmain's death, he succeeded as head designer of the house, where he stayed until 1990.*

GEOFFREY BEENE *(b. 1927), who hails from Haynesville, Louisiana, graduated from high school at the age of 16 and entered Tulane University's pre-med program on scholarship. Realizing that fashion was his true calling, he left to study at design academies in California, New York, and Paris (at the school of the Chambre Syndicale), serving a final apprenticeship with one of Captain Molyneux's tailors. Beene began his own company in 1963, and was soon recognized for his iconoclastic use of fabric, his technical brilliance, and the fierce focus of his modernist vision (Adrian and Schiaparelli, both great experimenters, were formative inspirations). Beene's* understanding of human form and motion, coupled with his fearless stress on the present tense, has made for a body of work that is uniquely coherent, inventive, evolving. His devoted following consists not just of the women who wear his clothes, but of artists and intellectuals, too.

COCO CHANEL *(1883–1971)*, born in Saumur, France, told conflicting stories of her childhood. What is known for sure is that by 1914 she opened hat shops in Paris and Deauville and then branched into sportswear, changing fashion forever with her chemises in knit jersey. She appropriated traditional menswear shapes and reproportioned them for women, creating a look of youthful elegance that depended less on buckets of money than on sleek good taste and imagination. In 1983 KARL LAGERFELD *(b. 1938)* took the reins at the house of Chanel. Lagerfeld was born in Hamburg to a family of industrialists. His first step in fashion was winning first prize in the International Wool Secretariat design contest; as a result, at the age of 17 he became an apprentice at Balmain. Lagerfeld quickly went from one success to another, designing for Jean Patou, Dunhill, Charles Jourdan, Fendi, Chloé, and for the opera and theater. Multilingual and a voracious reader, he seems to hold court at the center of the fashion whirl, and his ongoing romance with eras of the past, tempered by his hawk eye for the zeitgeist, keeps his work for Chanel ever influential.

CHRISTIAN DIOR *(1905–1957)* was born in Granville, Normandy. His early adult years were spent in search of the right career: he studied political science, music, and art. In 1935 Dior began selling fashion sketches to newspapers, and voilà, he found his focus. He went to work at Piguet in 1938, at Lelong in 1942, and in 1947 opened his own house with the legendary "New Look": a collection that put war-deprived women back into boned corsets and deeply tailored and flared suits and dresses. Each collection grew out of a distinct line—a stress on invention that was exhausting to maintain. Dior died after ten history-making years in his own house.

GIANFRANCO FERRÉ *(b. 1944)*, the Italian master of a company he had established in 1978, came to the house of Dior in 1989. Ferré was born in Legnano, Italy, and earned a degree in architecture from the Milan Polytechnic Institute. An interest in fashion led him to design a collection of jewelry and accessories, which was soon followed by a clothing line. Success was instant. A trip to India early in his career completed Ferré's aesthetic, teaching him that purity was the goal of all good design. Ferré's work shows the architect's sure hand with proportion and scale, enriched by an almost exotic sensuality.

At the age of 27, LOUIS FÉRAUD *(b. 1920)* settled down in Cannes, France, and began painting (and watching Westerns). His friendships with movie stars who visited the famous local film festival coincided with his foray into fashion design, and in 1955 he established the first couture house in Cannes, and one in Paris as well. He became known as the designer who dressed Brigitte Bardot in many movies. Féraud has continued to paint and to write novels throughout his design career, and he is particularly esteemed as a colorist whose work is influenced by the art of South America.

JAMES GALANOS *(b. 1924)* was born in Philadelphia and raised in New Jersey, the son of a restaurant owner from Greece. By the age of 14 he knew that he wanted to design clothes, and at

23 he apprenticed in Paris at the house of Piguet. Returning to the States, Galanos found New York's Seventh Avenue inhospitable and eventually set up shop in California, where he forged a reputation for meticulous craftsmanship that not only rivaled, but often bettered, that of Paris couture (his workrooms are staffed by women from European ateliers and the film studios of Hollywood). Famous for his cocktail dresses and evening clothes, his magical work with chiffon, and his hand-shaped wools, the name Galanos is synonymous with privileged perfection.

As a boy growing up in Beauvais, France, HUBERT DE GIVENCHY (b. 1927) was much influenced by his grandfather, who had been director of the Gobelin tapestry works. At the age of 10, he saw the Pavillon d'Elégance at the 1937 Paris Exposition, and his career was cast. After serving a string of apprenticeships at the houses of Fath, Piguet, Lelong, and Schiaparelli, Givenchy opened his own in house in 1952. In the beginning he worked with cotton because it was affordable, and he had a huge success with the white cotton, ruffled "Bettina blouse." Though he was soon able to work with the richest fabrics, he always retained his signature delicacy and restraint. Givenchy had two touchstone relationships. One was with Balenciaga, who in 1953 became a friend and mentor; allied on a fashion issue, these men were a formidable force. The second was with Audrey Hepburn, the actress Givenchy dressed in many film roles, and whose look enchanted the world, epitomizing Paris couture in the 1960s.

GIVENCHY WITH AUDREY HEPBURN, 1987.

CHARLES JAMES (1904 1978) was born and raised in London. After an early adulthood in Chicago working first in architectural design and then at a newspaper, he opened a hat shop in 1926. More hat shops followed, and soon he was designing ingenious dresses for a sterling clientele that included Millicent Rogers, Coco Chanel, and Diana Vreeland. Temperamental and litigious, James continually sabotaged his own success, but the lush, structural beauty of his designs really do have the quality of natural phenomena.

CHRISTIAN LACROIX (b. 1951) was born in Arles, France. His childhood was lonely, and he spent much of his time drawing, especially sketching historical costumes and creating his own fashion designs. He earned an arts degree, and in 1973 went to the Sorbonne to prepare a dissertation on seventeenth-century costume. Lacroix planned to be a museum curator, but friends, among them Karl Lagerfeld, encouraged him in his designing. In 1978 he began an apprenticeship

CHRISTIAN LACROIX WITH SABINE AZEMA, 1987.

with Hermès, and in 1982 became head of design at Jean Patou, where he made his name with an exuberant 1986 collection. Belle Epoque poufs, rousing ethnic colors, and exquisite construction became the Lacroix signature. He launched his own house the following year with another stunning collection, and won such immediate acclaim that many fans compared the debut to Dior's.

The house of Lanvin is now the oldest in Paris, established in 1890 by JEANNE LANVIN (1867 - 1946). Lanvin first designed hats, then children's clothes that charmed mothers, and then similarly charming dresses for adults. She broke with the turn-of-the-century tradition of rigidly dressing one's age. A Lanvin dress or gown was characterized by its prettiness, its soft, silvery palette of pinks and periwinkle blues, and a penchant for appliqué and embroidery. Nature, flowers, plants, and paintings were her inspiration.

flowers, plants, and paintings were her inspiration. CLAUDE MONTANA (b. 1949) became fully established in the world of haute couture when he designed five award-winning collections for Lanvin from 1989 to 1991. Born in Paris of German and Spanish parents, Montana went to London to seek his fortune and was applauded for jewelry he made from papier-mâché. He also began to design in leather—spectacularly—and from there went on to success as a designer of ready-to-wear and boutique lines.

Born in La Rochelle, France, GUY LAROCHE (1923–1989) went to Paris at a young age and began work with a milliner. He continued in the millinery trade after World War II, working for two years in New York on Seventh Avenue. Returning to Paris, Laroche took a job at Dessès. He worked there for eight years, and in 1957 was ready to begin his own company. Fine cutting and tailoring were Laroche trademarks, with the stress on sportswear.

NORMAN NORELL (1900–1972) was born in Noblesville, Indiana, son of a haberdasher. His ambition was to be an artist, and at age 19 he went to New York to study at Parsons School of Design and then at the Pratt Institute. Putting the "Nor" in Norman together with the "L" from his surname, Levinson, he became Norell and started designing costumes for Paramount Pictures in New York. During the 1920s he also did costumes for the Ziegfeld Follies and the Cotton Club. Through the 1930s Norell worked for the firm of Anthony Traina, renamed Traina-Norell. When Traina retired in 1960, the label and company became Norell's. Though his clothes were technically ready-to-wear, a Norell was distinguished by superb craftsmanship, quality fabric, and simple yet arresting design. Every detail was functional and luxurious.

PAUL POIRET (1879–1944), whose first apprenticeship was with an umbrella maker, began sketching dress designs as an escape from the job's tedium. He sold sketches to the great couture houses until Jacques Doucet took him on as a protégé. Work with Worth followed, and Poiret opened his own house in 1914—his Empire sheaths instantly dating the hourglass figure. Consciously artistic, Poiret's house made room for budding talents such as Erté and Raoul Dufy. ERTÉ (1892–1990), who spent a year with Poiret and then left to work with Diaghilev on theater and ballet decor, would become a world-famous set and costume designer.

Born in Turin, Italy, NINA RICCI (1883–1970) was apprenticed to a dressmaker by the age of 13. By age 22 she was chief designer. Together with her husband, a jeweler, she opened her own house in 1932; eventually her son, Robert, became the official director. Like Vionnet, Ricci took a hands-on approach to design, working the fabric around the body of a living model. Her designs could be daring in the way they attracted attention to the female form, but they were always inherently tasteful and feminine. At the request of Robert Ricci, Paris-born GÉRARD PIPART (b. 1933) took over as designer for the house of Ricci in 1964, arriving with a background of superb work at Balmain, Fath, and Patou, as well as free-lance work in ready-to-wear for many houses.

Born in Oran, Algeria, YVES SAINT LAURENT (b. 1936) was an extremely sensitive child whose interest in fashion was quickened by seeing a production of Molière's School for Wives.

its sets and costumes designed by Christian Bérard. At age 17 Saint Laurent won first prize in the International Wool Secretariat contest. After only months of study at the school of the Chambre Syndicale, he became an assistant to Christian Dior, and his precocious designs were incorporated into Dior's final collections. Upon Dior's death, Saint Laurent took over—with great success at first. But as he pushed his vision to the cutting edge, Dior's conservative following balked. Conscription into the army forced his separation from the house. Saint Laurent returned to Paris and opened his own house; collections were based less on a seasonal "line" than on the evocation of an era or ideal (the Ballets Russes, the gypsies of Carmen). A YSL suit is a special silhouette: sharply scaled to the eternal feminine.

ARNOLD SCAASI (b. 1931), whose surname is "Isaacs" spelled backward, was born in Montreal and raised both there and in Melbourne, Australia. A precocious student with inborn originality, Scaasi whipped through design school in Montreal and then enrolled at the school of the Chambre Syndicale in Paris. After apprenticeship at the house of Paquin and then with Charles James in New York, he set out on his own in 1957 and quickly made his name with sumptuous, often flamboyant, evening gowns. Scaasi dresses stars and society—and has also designed for at least four first ladies.

Born in Paris, JEAN-LOUIS SCHERRER (b. 1936) was a dancer until a fall sidelined him at the age of 20. He took up sketching and then worked side by side with Yves Saint Laurent at the house of Dior. When the master died and Saint Laurent took over as head designer, Scherrer left to open his own house. In 1962 his first collection was shown in the vaulted cellar of a wine dealer. After one season he could already count as clients names like Baroness Von Thyssen and Françoise Sagan, women attracted to Scherrer's disciplined cutting and extravagant evening gowns.

ELSA SCHIAPARELLI (1890–1973) was born in Rome, daughter of well-to-do, academic parents who found her imagination all too daring. Paris in the 1930s, however, was ready for sensation, and Schiaparelli provided it, starting with a modest success in 1928: a black-and-white wool sweater with a bow knitted in. From trompe l'oeil she went on to surrealism and futurism, making her suits and evening gowns canvases for Cocteau, Bérard, and Dali, as well as mediums of avant-garde experimentation in the use of devices (like zippers) and newly developed materials (like Viyella and Rhodophane, a glass fabric). Schiaparelli dressed strong, stylish women—from Marlene Dietrich to Wallis Simpson. Her house closed in 1954, ending her witty run of surprising and delightful design.

EMANUEL UNGARO (b. 1933) could work a sewing machine from the age of 5. Born in Aix-en-Provence, France, to Italian parents, he was brought up in the family tailoring business. He went to Paris in 1955 and three years later landed his dream job: work with Balenciaga. After six years with the master, he moved to Courrèges for

EMANUEL UNGARO WITH ANOUK AIMÉE, 1987.

two seasons and then set out on his own in 1965, presenting his first collection of twenty models in a small Paris apartment, each item personally cut, fitted, and sewn by him. A star was born. Ungaro was at the center of that space-age era of short skirts, silvered accessories, and sharp edges, but over the years he has become famous for his bold prints (which he mixes with panache) and ultra-feminine dresses worn by an international clientele.

Born in Rome to a wealthy and supportive family, VALENTINO GARAVANI (b. 1933) began learning French as a boy, already aware that he'd need the language for his chosen career.

He moved to Paris in 1950 to study at the Ecole des Beaux-Arts and the school of the Chambre Syndicale. He then apprenticed with Jean Dessès and Guy Laroche. Returning to Rome, Valentino opened his first atelier, financed by his father. It was in 1967, however, that Valentino made his unforgettable mark: in the midst of the Peter Max 1960s, he presented a "no color" collection of designs in shades of white, ivory, cream, etc. The impact was enormous, and Valentino entered the ranks of couture's elite, a status he's enjoyed ever since, dressing jet-set women from Jacqueline Kennedy Onassis to Elizabeth Taylor. Indeed, a Valentino wedding dress may be the ultimate symbol of high society.

PHILIPPE VENET (b. 1929) was born in Lyons, France. At age 14 he apprenticed with Pierre Court, a couturier based in Lyons, and he reached Paris in 1951, working first for Schiaparelli and then, a year later, for Givenchy. Venet opened his own house in 1962 and is famous for coats and dresses of pure, seemingly conservative design and impeccable, beautiful tailoring. He is the couturier of the understated aristocrat.

Born in Calabria, Italy, GIANNI VERSACE (b. 1946) learned from and was inspired by his mother, who was a dressmaker. From an early age he helped her by searching out new stones, beads, and braids to give to the embroiderer. As a young man in Milan, Versace designed suede and leather collections for Genny and evening clothes for Complice. He presented his first fashion collection in 1978, and his first Atelier collection in Paris in 1989, also designing costumes for the theater, opera, and ballet. It's no surprise that one of

Versace's hallmarks as a designer is the lavish embroidery he uses both as serious decoration and as ironic overstatement. There has always been something of the colorful court jester about Versace, who juggles the classical and the iconoclastic often within the same design, and delights in creating street chic of couture quality.

MADELEINE VIONNET (1876–1975) went to work as an apprentice seamstress at the age of 12, graduated to the couture houses of London and Paris, and opened her own house in 1912. Head of a quiet revolution, Vionnet simultaneously dispensed with corsets and honored the female figure by inventing the bias-cut dress. She designed with her hands, modeling fabric on miniature mannequins, and favored flowing fabrics in "off" shades. Today, Vionnets are valued as masterpieces.

A native of New York born to parents who fled the Chinese Revolution, VERA WANG (b. 1949) originally dreamed of triumph as an Olympic figure skater. When she did not make the team in 1968 she left skating and went to the Sorbonne and then to Sarah Lawrence College, forbidden by her parents to go to design school. Wang then became the youngest editor ever at Vogue magazine, where she stayed for seventeen years. Next, she became design director at Ralph Lauren. In 1990 Wang opened a bridal house and a made-to-order salon, her specialty being uniquely flattering gowns, both bridal and evening. Wang won international prominence when she costumed figure skater Nancy Kerrigan in the 1994 Winter Olympics. Illusion netting and a pared-away, body-hugging fit are Wang's forte.

SELECTED BIBLIOGRAPHY

Bertin, Célia. Paris à la Mode. New York: Harper and Brothers, 1957.

Boucher, François. 20,000 Years of Fashion. New York: Harry N. Abrams, 1965.

Dariaux, Geneviève Antoine. Elegance. Garden City, N.Y.: Doubleday & Company, 1964.

Fairchild, John. The Fashionable Savages. Garden City, N.Y.: Doubleday & Company, 1965.

Jouve, Marie-Andrée, and Jacqueline Demornex. Balenciaga. New York: Rizzoli International, 1989.

Kennan, Brigid. Dior in Vogue. New York: Harmony Books, 1981.

Kennett, Frances. Secrets of the Couturiers. New York: Exeter Books, 1984.

Lambert, Eleanor. World of Fashion. New York: R. R. Bowker Company, 1976.

Lynam, Ruth. Couture. Garden City, N.Y.: Doubleday & Company, 1972.

Milbank, Caroline Rennolds. Couture. New York: Stewart, Tabori & Chang, 1985.

Mulvagh, Jane. Vogue History of 20th Century Fashion. London and New York: Viking, 1988.

O'Hara, Georgina. The Encyclopedia of Fashion. New York: Harry N. Abrams, 1986.

Pellé, Marie-Paule, with Patrick Mauriès. Valentino: Thirty Years of Magic. New York: Abbeville Press, 1990.

Versace, Gianni. Vanitas: Designs. New York: Abbeville Press, 1994.

INDEX